The Great Corn Invention

Written by Mary-Anne Creasy

Illustrated by Steve Axelsen

Flying Start
to Literacy®

Contents

Chapter 1

The Cornville Inventors Club

Ben, Anna and Maria lived in Cornville. The three children had their own club – The Inventors Club – and they met each week to work on their inventions. Ben's dad let them use his old, cluttered shed as their clubhouse.

"We really need a proper clubhouse," Maria sighed at the weekly meeting, squashed between boxes and gardening tools in the corner of the shed.

"Yeah, we need more space to build our inventions," said Anna.

"Well, the Cornville Corn Festival is next month," Ben said. "And there's prize money to be won for the best inventions!"

The children's eyes lit up, and they all looked at each other and smiled. That's how they'd get the money for their new clubhouse!

"And," Maria chimed in, "I've heard that King Corn himself will be presenting the prizes!"

The Cornville Corn Festival was the biggest corn festival in the world. People came from everywhere to eat corn, talk about corn and enter the competitions for new corn inventions.

King Corn was the biggest buyer of corn in the town. His factory produced tinned corn, cornmeal, popcorn and more. Every year, King Corn came to the festival to look at new corn products. He was also interested in new ways to grow corn, protect it from pests and harvest it.

But nobody in Cornville knew what King Corn looked like – he always attended the festival in secret.

Chapter 2

Preparing for competition

The day before the Cornville Corn Festival, the members of The Inventors Club were busy finishing their inventions.

"How's everyone going?" asked Maria, as it began to get dark outside.

"Mine's almost ready," called Ben, tightening a bolt on a mechanical arm.

"What about yours, Anna?" he asked.

"Just a few more adjustments, and it's done," said Anna. "How about you, Maria? How's the corn coming along?"

"Um, yeah, it's great," said Maria, looking nervous.

"It is going to be ready, isn't it?" asked Ben. "Can we see it?"

"No, no!" Maria answered quickly. "Um, the corn will be ruined if it's exposed to the light. It will be ready though, I promise."

The Inventors Club arrived at the cornfield
early to set up their inventions. The festival
was held in a different cornfield each year.
A big area of corn was cut down and
harvested to clear a spot for the festival,
but tall stalks still stood in the nearby fields.

"We're going to win the prize money, I just
know it," said Ben.

"And maybe we'll get to meet King Corn!"
said Anna. "I wonder who he is ..."

"Look, there's the Mayor with someone now,"
said Maria.

The Mayor of Cornville was talking to a big, red-faced man who was munching on a corn cob. The Mayor put his arm around the red-faced man and, as they came closer, the children saw something glint in the sunlight.

"He's wearing a gold corn badge, just like the Mayor's!" said Maria.

"And the Mayor is showing him around," added Anna. "He must be King Corn!"

"Come on, let's get our inventions ready," Ben said. "We have to win that prize!"

Chapter 3
Covered in corn

A few hours later, the crowds waited for the competitions for corn inventions to begin.

"The first competition is for the best corn-picking machine," the Mayor announced. "Teams, get into position. Get ready to start up your machines."

Ben pulled the cover off his invention and the crowd gasped. There stood a harvesting machine with big, mechanical arms.

"Excuse me," came a quiet voice from behind Ben. "Can I have a look at that machine?"

Ben turned around to see a pale man
in a long, grey coat.

"Not now," said Ben. "The competition is
about to start."

"Ready! Set! Go!" said the Mayor.

Ben pushed the button and his machine started up. It worked perfectly. As it rolled slowly between the corn stalks, the mechanical hands picked the corn gently and dropped the corn cobs into a basket.

But quite suddenly, the machine began moving faster and faster. The mechanical hands were out of control. They crushed the cobs into a pulpy mess and threw them at the crowd! The Mayor and the red-faced man were covered in milky corn juice, kernels and husks.

"Turn that machine off!" yelled the Mayor.

Ben ran after the machine and quickly pressed the button to stop it.

"I'm sorry," said Ben to the Mayor and the red-faced man. "I don't know what went wrong."

The pale man in the long, grey coat went up to the machine. "I think you've over-tightened the bolts, here and here," he said to Ben, pointing to one of the hands.

"Oh, yes," said Ben. "Thanks." Ben felt really embarrassed at what had happened. Everyone was busy cleaning and comforting the Mayor and the red-faced man.

Chapter 4
Corn surprise

"The next competition is for the best popcorn machine," said the Mayor.

When it was her turn, Anna flung the cover off her machine and looked up at the cloudless sky.

"Well, what are we waiting for?" asked the Mayor.

"We have to wait for it to heat up," said
Anna. "It's a solar-powered popcorn machine."

The Mayor laughed and nudged the
red-faced man. "We'll be here all day!"

Suddenly, a popping sound came from the
machine. Anna clapped excitedly.
"It's working!"

"Well, I'm hungry. When will it be ready?"
asked the red-faced man. "And where's the
butter?" Then he stopped and sniffed the
air. "I smell burning," he said.

The machine was shaking. There was a loud bang and the lid flew off, sending flaming balls of popcorn into the field nearby. A farmer started frantically filling buckets of water and yelling, "My cornfield is on fire! Help, help!"

The pale man in the long, grey coat approached Anna. "Excuse me," he said. "I think I see the problem with your machine." He pointed to the solar panels. "They're too big. They create too much heat."

"Oh," said Anna sadly. "That makes sense. Thank you."

Meanwhile, the Mayor was very angry. "That's it! You children are banned from competing at the Cornville Corn Festival for life!" he shouted, as he and the others stormed off.

The pale man in the long, grey coat turned to Maria. "Do you have an invention, too?" he asked.

"Yes," Maria said sadly, pointing to her pots of corn on a table nearby. "I grew these for the novelty corn competition."

Maria went over, picked an ear of her corn and slowly peeled back the husk. "Oh, no!" she cried.

The man picked up the cob. "What's wrong?" he asked.

"It's meant to be pink," wailed Maria. "And look at it, it's orange!"

"Well, orange is my favourite colour," said the pale man in the long, grey coat, taking a bite. "Mmm," he said, shutting his eyes. "Mmmmm! That's amazing. This is the sweetest corn I've ever tasted. It's sweet and juicy and crunchy!"

Maria took a bite. "I guess it is pretty sweet," she said.

"Not only that," said the man. "I think this corn can be eaten straight from the stalk – no cooking!" He walked away, laughing to himself, picking another ear of Maria's corn as he went.

Chapter 5
An unexpected visitor

The next day at The Inventors Club meeting, Ben and Anna were testing their inventions again.

"Wow," said Anna, "I've made these solar panels smaller and now the popcorn machine works perfectly!"

"And I've loosened these bolts and my harvesting machine works much better," said Ben. "That man in the long, grey coat sure did know his stuff."

Maria sat outside, looking sadly at her corn. "It should have been pink," she was saying to herself when she was startled by Ben.

"Wow, look at that car!" he shouted. A long, orange car pulled up and the pale man in the long, grey coat got out.

"Hello, kids," he said to them. "How are The Inventors Club members today?"

They looked at each other. Then Maria spoke. "Not so good. Our inventions weren't exactly a success."

"And we're banned from competing at the Cornville Corn Festival for life!" said Ben.

The man chuckled. "Inventors always have a tough time. You just have to keep trying."

"I'm an inventor, too," said the man. "Well, I used to be. Now I own a factory. My name is King Corn."

"King Corn!" said the kids all at once.

"But we thought the red-faced man was King Corn," said Maria.

"Oh, no, that was the mayor of another town," said King Corn. "The Mayor of Cornville wants to sell him the Cornville Corn Festival idea to take to his own town."

"So there would be no more Cornville Corn Festival?" asked Anna.

"That's right," said King Corn, laughing. "But you did a great job to stop that from happening! I think everyone in town will be very grateful."

"But I'm not here to talk about the Cornville Corn Festival," King Corn continued. "I'm here to buy your idea."

"Which one?" said Ben. "My harvesting machine?"

"My popcorn machine?" asked Anna.

King Corn shook his head. "It's Maria's sweet, delicious corn I want to buy." He pulled an orange cob out of his pocket.

Maria's eyes lit up, but the others looked at the corn cob in surprise.

"It's orange!" said Ben. "You said it would be pink."

"There's nothing wrong with orange," said King Corn. "Sometimes an inventor's best invention is the one they discover by chance."

The Inventors Club agreed that orange corn was definitely Maria's best invention – after all, it paid for their brand new, bright orange clubhouse!

A note from the author

When I was trying to think of a story about corn, I first read about the history of corn. I discovered that it is a huge part of American agriculture and vital to many communities. These communities celebrate the importance of corn with corn festivals.

I found out that over time there have been many new ways of picking corn and using corn, as well as new types of corn. During my research, I saw photos of beautiful coloured corn. We often hear about inventions of machines and technology, but food inventions are less common, so I thought it would be interesting to make Maria's new type of corn the most important invention of all.